# Psalm Book

**Presented to**

_____

**By**

_____

**On**

_____

# Psalm Book

## Prayers and Poems for Kids

Edited by
Naomi J. Krueger
★
Illustrated by
Peter Grosshauser

**Written by**

Judy Beglau

Micha Boyett

Lisa Marie Brodsky Auter

Jennifer Grant

Carol Hegberg

Cathy M. Kolwey

Claudia Rosemary May

Cathy Skogen-Soldner

Michelle Van Loon

SPARK
HOUSE
FAMILY
MINNEAPOLIS

First edition published 2016
Printed in the United States of America
22  21  20  19  18  17          2  3  4  5  6  7  8

Edited by Naomi J. Krueger
Written by Judy Beglau, Micha Boyett, Lisa Marie Brodsky Auter, Jennifer Grant, Cathy M. Kolwey, Carol Hegberg, Claudia Rosemary May, Cathy Skogen-Soldner, Michelle Van Loon
Designed by Mighty Media
Illustrated by Peter Grosshauser

Library of Congress Cataloging-in-Publication Data

Names: Beglau, Judy, author. | Krueger, Naomi J., editor. | Grosshauser, Peter, illustrator.
Title: Spark Story Bible Psalm book : prayers and poems for kids / written by Judy Beglau [and 8 others] ; edited by Naomi J. Krueger ; illustrated by Peter Grosshauser.
Other titles: Bible Psalm book | Psalm book
Description: Minneapolis, MN : Sparkhouse Family, [2016] | Audience: Ages 5-8. | Audience: K to grade 3.
Identifiers: LCCN 2016006495 (print) | LCCN 2016012788 (ebook) | ISBN 9781506417684 (hardcover : alk. paper) | ISBN 9781506417790 (E-Book)
Subjects: LCSH: Bible. Psalms--Juvenile literature. | Children--Prayers and devotions--Juvenile literature. | Children--Religious life--Juvenile literature. | Christian poetry--Juvenile literature.
Classification: LCC BS551.3 .S6345 2016 (print) | LCC BS551.3 (ebook) | DDC
    242.62--dc23
LC record available at http://lccn.loc.gov/2016006495

VN0004589; 9781506417684; AUG2017

Sparkhouse Family
510 Marquette Avenue
Minneapolis, MN 55402
sparkhouse.org

# Contents

## Prayers of
## Morning and Evening

## Prayers of Praise

## Prayers of Comfort

# Prayers of Creation

# A Message for Kids

Welcome to the *Spark Story Bible Psalm Book*! The prayers in this book can help you find words to talk to God when you're not sure what to say. The poems and prayers in this book were inspired by the book of Psalms in the Bible. You can find the book of Psalms in the Old Testament, about halfway through the Bible.

The psalms (pronounced SALMS) are a collection of songs, prayers, and poems to God. They express all kinds of human emotions: joy, sadness, anger, fear, thankfulness, and more!

For thousands of years, people have sung songs and prayed prayers based on the words of the psalms.

The psalms were written by kings, leaders, and ordinary people like us. Many of the psalms were written with King David in mind. Maybe you've heard about the little boy who fought the giant? That's David! Later in his life he became one of the most famous kings in the history of Israel, and he is also one of Jesus' ancestors.

Find a quiet spot in your home or outside. Take a deep breath. Page through this book and find a prayer that fits your mood. Read it out loud or quietly in your heart. God hears you no matter what!

Blessings,
The Sparkhouse Family Team

# A Message for Grown-Ups

Welcome to the *Spark Story Bible Psalm Book*!

Even though the psalms are thousands of years old, they still speak to us. The psalms are filled with raw emotion, giving us a beautiful example of what it looks like to come to God with our greatest joys and our greatest needs. The psalms help children discover that they can come to God with all their highs and lows, their joy and sadness. They can start the day with the promise of God's presence and snuggle in for the night with the assurance of God's protection.

As you and your child pray these prayers, you will join in with one of the oldest traditions of God's people. Jesus frequently quoted the psalms to remind his listeners of God's long-standing promises. Today, churches around the world read and sing the psalms every week.

Each prayer in this book is written as a poem in child-friendly language and is based on a central element of the selected psalm. We encourage you to read and pray with your child, using this book to guide your prayers, whether it's at bedtime, at mealtimes, or just because.

Older children might enjoy reading the prayers alongside the original psalms in the Bible. You can even expand your child's prayer life by encouraging them to write their own versions of the psalms or to come up with prayers based on the four categories in this book: Prayers of Morning and Evening, Prayers of Praise, Prayers of Comfort, and Prayers of Creation.

We hope this *Spark Story Bible Psalm Book* will inspire you and your children as you bring your praises, worries, frustrations, and joys to God.

Blessings,
The Sparkhouse Family Team

# Prayers of Morning and Evening

# Your Warm Love

*A Prayer from Psalm 5*

••

Good morning, Lord.

I'm here to ask for just one thing.

Will you be my safe place?

When I am afraid, I will take shelter in your love.

I know that you listen

and will gladly take care of us.

Like a big blanket,

spread out your loving arms

to cover and protect us.

Wrapped in your care,

people everywhere celebrate

your warm love together.

17

# First Song of the Day

*A Prayer from Psalm 57*

••

I could sit around and talk about people
in my life who are like lions,
with their sharp teeth and mean words; but no . . .
I am going to make music for you, God!
The best way to start my day is
by bursting into joyful song,
or blowing all of my air into the trumpet,
or sweeping my hands over the
strings of the harp—
all in praise to you!

My first song of the day will tell
people all over the world
that your love is the greatest love—
perfect in every way.
And your friendship is impossible to measure,
even higher than the sky!
I just can't help myself—
I will sing and make music for you!

# You Are Wonderful!

*A Prayer from Psalm 113*

••

You deserve our thank-yous when the sun pops up.
You deserve our wows when the sun slides down.

Morning and night, in the light and the darkness,
right now and forever, you are wonderful!

What is beyond the stars and planets,
the black holes and swirling galaxies?
Only you, God! You are bigger than our
dreams and as close as our breath.

You come to the sad and the lonely,
to those who say: *There is no hope.*
You turn their stories right side up.
You give them joy and friends and courage.

You are a miracle-worker, Lord!

# Your Love

*A Prayer from Psalm 108*

••

As high as the sky,
streaked with morning's dawn . . .
is your love.
As loud as the crashing waves
against the solid earth . . .
is your love.
As long as the journey
of eons of starlight . . .
is your love.

I will wake up the whole world praising you, God!

You have poured into me
all the love of your heart
and made me your precious child.
Hear my voice singing to you,
and keep me with you always.
Call my name when I forget
that you are my truth, my safety, my friend.

# My Soul Is Like the Dawn

*A Prayer from Psalm 131*

••

My soul breathes peace.
It is like the night
when darkness drapes the sky
and the sun sleeps
and silence fills my home.
My mind rests in quiet.

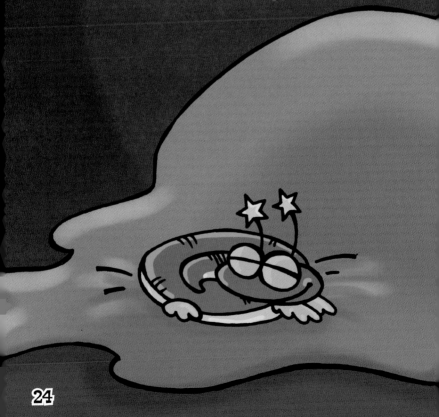

My soul breathes peace.
It is like the dawn
when the sun wakes up.
It awakens my mind and body.

My soul is content with you, God.
Like the embrace of a mother,
you comfort me from within.

# When Tears Fall

*A Prayer from Psalm 22*

••

God, why aren't you with me?
I look for you everywhere
and don't see you nearby.
All day my tears fall; I can't hear your voice.
The night is quiet, and I cannot sleep.
But even in quiet and even in night,
you are bigger than sadness or fear!
My Lord, my friend, you won't leave my side.
I'm strong when you're here—
all day and all night.

# Keep Me Safe

*A Prayer from Psalm 3*

••

God, thank you for protecting me!
You shield me on all sides.
When I cry myself to sleep,
your big hand is my pillow.
You answer my prayers from your holy hill.
I will not be afraid.
You stay with me through the night.
Tomorrow morning I will awake
and have your blessing.

# My Heart Listens for You

*A Prayer from Psalm 16*

••

Keep me safe tonight, God.

Your Spirit lives in my heart.

I praise you for your guidance.

Even at night my heart listens for you.
I will fear nothing,
because you are beside me.

My heart is happy.
I sing beautiful songs about you.
You lead me where I should go,
and I am joyful from knowing you are with me.

# Like a Mama Bird

*A Prayer from Psalm 91*

••

God, I can come to you
and find a safe place to hide
when scary things are happening all around me.

You'll protect me just as a mama bird
protects her babies in a storm.
She spreads her wings over them like an umbrella
and keeps her little ones warm and dry.

Dear Lord, I am so glad I can talk to you anytime:
in the morning when the little birds are singing,
in the afternoon when the rain is
pounding against the roof,
or in the nighttime darkness.
You hear my prayers—all the time and always.

# I Can't Sleep

### A Prayer from Psalm 77

••

I woke up scared and screaming,
and I can't go back to sleep.
I prayed for good dreams,
and all I had were nightmares.
I lie awake and wonder,
*Do you want to help me, God?*
*Are your promises real?*

When I can't sleep, I list the things I love.
I remember your gifts to me:
I imagine the fresh sweet smell of rainstorms,
the song of your booming thunder.
I think of running into ocean waves,
salt water and sand on my feet.

I think of the creatures I love:
dolphins and whale sharks,
porcupine puffer fish, sea stars and jellies.

I close my eyes and thank you
for making things I love.
I remember that you know my name!
You love me because you made me too.

# Watching Over Me

*A Prayer from Psalm 121*

••

My eyes look up higher than
the mountains and hills, asking:
*Who will help me?*
My help comes from you who made everything—
the sky and the earth!

You won't let me fall—
you stay awake at my bedside,
and while I sleep you never close your eyes.
You are my great night-light.

I will trust in you.
You are my God who watches over me forever.

# In the Shadow of Your Heart

*A Prayer from Psalm 63*

••

When I think about you,
I sometimes long to see your face.
I want to feel your arms around me
and always keep you close.

Sometimes I feel far away from you.

I feel thirsty, lost and alone in a dry desert.

But then you come to me,

pouring out your love like cool water.

At night in my bed,

I am safe in the shadow of your heart

and I can sleep in peace.

Always and forever

I will sing to you with joy, my God.

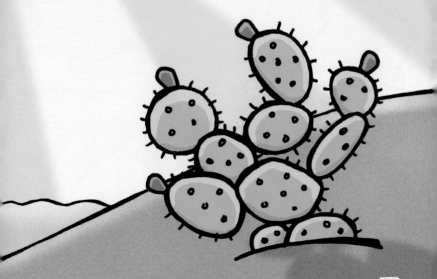

# Prayers of Praise

# I Give You Praise

*A Prayer from Psalm 47*

My whole being wants
to rejoice about you,
Creator God.
If everyone in the whole world
stopped right now
and sang songs to you,
we'd sing about how generous
and kind you are
and how very special you are—
you're holy and mysterious.

I feel amazed and happy
when I think about you.
I give you praise,
King of all.

# Thank You for Healing Me

*A Prayer from Psalm 30*

••

Thank you, God, for healing me.
I prayed to you when I was sick,
and you made me well!
I am not sad anymore.
I felt like I was in a deep hole,
and I cried at night.

—

Then in the morning,
I was full of joy.
You turned my weeping
into dancing.
You clothed me
with happiness.
Now my heart sings to you.
I will praise you always!

# I Love You So

*A Prayer from Psalm 67*

••

The warm light of your love

shines on my face

and fills my heart with joy.

Help me always remember

to call out to you, to give you thanks,

to live the way you have told me is best.


Then all people all over the world

will see your goodness

and feel your loving power

and sing with one loud voice,

"You are my God, and I love you so."

## In Your House

*A Prayer from Psalm 84*

• •

How lovely is your house, O God!
My soul wants to be with you,
where the sparrow and the
swallow have their nests.
I will set my heart on a journey
to learn about you.
In good and bad times, you give me courage.

Better is one day in your house
than a thousand any other place.

I would rather be with you all the time
than be anywhere else, God.
You shelter and protect me.
I am happy, because I trust in you.

49

# Dance, Sing, and Shout!

*A Prayer from Psalm 33*

••

I clap my hands.

I stamp my feet.

I dance with my whole body.

I dance!

I sing with my whole heart.

I sing!

I sing a brand new song

from the top of my lungs,

because you are wonderful.

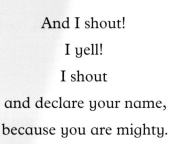

And I shout!
I yell!
I shout
and declare your name,
because you are mighty.

I beat my drum.
I play the cymbals.
I blow a trumpet.
I march up and down
the yard,
the street,
the field.
I sing my love songs to you—
I rejoice in you,
because you are awesome.

# I Will Praise You Always

*A Prayer from Psalm 146*

••

God, I will praise you all of my life!

Why will I praise you?
Because I know you are
the maker of *everything*—
sky and earth, land and seas,
and all the creatures
that live in them.
You care for me
and for all of creation
throughout time and forever.

Why will I praise you?

Because I know you care for every one of us.

The happy, the sad, the poor,

the rich, the healthy, and the sick.

You love everyone everywhere.

I will praise you always.

# We're Giving You a Party!

*A Prayer from Psalm 95*

••

God, we're giving you a party!

We sing JOY for you!

We shout *THANK YOU*

and dance a huge WOW!

We celebrate all you created!

So MIGHTY are your hands—
they reached deep down and formed the earth.
So HIGH is your reach—
you made the tall, majestic mountains.

Everything is yours!
Oh thank you, Father God, thank you Maker.

You are our leader, our shepherd,
and we are the sheep in your tender care.

# How Happy I Am

*A Prayer from Psalm 100*

••

With every living creature on the earth,
I shout with joy because you love me, God!
From the tips of my toes to the top of my head,
from the laugh in my belly
to the words on my tongue,
I sing with the giant wind
that blows round the world,
and I come to tell you how much I love you.
You made me, and your tender mercy covers me
like the love of a shepherd for his lamb,
forever and always!

How happy I am that you are my God!

# I Will Praise You

*A Prayer from Psalm 103*

••

Every single part of me—
from my head to my toes
and everything inside me—
praises you.

Your name is holy!

When I play,
I will praise you.
When I skip,
I will praise you.
When I do cartwheels,
I will praise you.
When I lie down,
I will praise you.
When I sit,
I will praise you.

Your name is holy!

# A God Who Rescues

*A Prayer from Psalm 105*

••

You are a God who rescues!

You freed the children of Israel
when the Egyptians forced them into slavery.
You made these weary, brokenhearted people
joyful again.

You are a God of miracles!

When your people were thirsty,
you made water come rushing out of rocks.
It splashed and puddled in dry desert sands.

You are a God who loves to bring
your children safely home!

You brought the children of Israel home
to a new, beautiful country,
and you bring me safely home every single day.

Thank you for taking such good care
of your people, including me.

# Always and Forever

*A Prayer from Psalm 136*

••

Lord, I can't measure
your love and great kindness.
It goes on and on—always and forever!

Instead of trying to measure, I think about
all the wonderful things you've done:
you made earth, sky, and sea,
you rescue people from harm,
and you lead them into sweet freedom!
As I remember, I overflow with thanks,
because you set me free to follow you.

You love each person perfectly—
I am amazed by you.
And when the world feels big and I feel small,
I remember you and know you are here.
Thank you, dear God, for being
with me—always and forever!

# You Never Leave My Side

*A Prayer from Psalm 139*

••

O Heavenly Papa,
Your light shines inside me.
You know everything about me—
everything!

You know what I am thinking;
you know when I am sad or angry or happy.
Wherever I go, you know where I am.
You created every part of me,
and you never leave my side.

Before I can think of what to say,
before words dance on my tongue,
you know how I will speak.
You always watch over me;
you never leave my side.

When I think about how you love and care for me,
when I think about how you want to be my friend,
and when I think about
how you never want to leave me,
I smile and I say,
*Thank you.*

# Whisper, Sing, and Shout

*A Prayer from Psalm 145*

••

The stories of God's goodness
are passed from one person to the next.
Families pass the stories down
to children and grandchildren.
Now it is my turn to add a
chapter to this joyful story:

Lord, you are slow to anger and quick to forgive.

What you say, you will do.

You keep your promises.

You are close to everyone who calls to you.

I want to whisper, sing, and shout

to the whole world:

Your love is wonderful, God!

# Praise You in Every Way

*A Prayer from Psalm 150*

••

God, I will praise you in every way:
with blaring trumpet or thumping timpani,
with plucky banjo or singing harp,
with wallowing bassoon or trilling flute,
with warm French horn or bright violin,
with booming tuba or clanging cymbals,
with marimba or djembe or ukulele,
with xylophone or accordion or castanets.
I will praise you in my loudest voice
or with any instrument I choose;
God, I will praise you in every way,
and I will praise you every day!

# Prayers of
# Comfort

# Help Me!

*A Prayer from Psalm 10*

••

God, sometimes when trouble
and troublemakers are all around me,
you seem far, far away.
And when you seem far away,
I get scared.

I feel alone and helpless.
Help me out!
I know you are listening.
Come and cheer me on!

# I Cry Out to You

*A Prayer from Psalm 18*

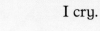

When sadness sits on my eyelids,

I cry out to you.

When worry stands on my shoulders,

I cry out to you.

When fear grips my mind,

I cry out to you.

When night clouds my view,

I cry out to you.

When thoughts silence my tongue,

I cry.

From anywhere in the world,
you hear my cries.
You kneel down and pull me out of raging waves.
You scoop me up into your arms
and cradle me.

You lead me to a place
where green grass fills my vision.
You hold my hand.
We walk together.
And when you look at me,
delight dances in your eyes.

# Like a Shepherd Lead Me

*A Prayer from Psalm 23*

••

Like a shepherd, Lord, please lead me.
Like a sheep, I need your guidance too.
Lead me to quiet waters and to green grass
where I can play.
When I am in dark and scary places,
watch over me and see me through.
It comforts me to know that
you will always keep me safe.
Pour your blessings over me, Lord,
and shower me with your grace.
That way I will have goodness and mercy
with me at all times.
Because you are my guide in life,
I will always be in your care.

# Safest Hiding Place

*A Prayer from Psalm 27*

••

Bullies try to push me around.
They treat me like I'm a piece of old trash
or the leftovers from yesterday's lunch.
They use hurtful words to try to make me feel
small, smaller, smallest!

Dear Lord, I can run to you.
You are the safest hiding place on earth.
You teach me how to be strong and kind,
just like you are.
When I am with you, I become
brave, braver, bravest!

# Will You Forgive Me?

*A Prayer from Psalm 32*

••

God, will you forgive me?

I know if I ask, you'll erase all my mistakes.
You know what is deep down in my heart,
so I share my problems with you
and don't hide them.

You know every mistake I've ever
made, and you forgive me.
Thank you!

You are my snuggling place.
You protect me from trouble and surround me
with soothing songs of your mighty power,
your long-lasting love, and your sweet forgiveness.
Thank you!

# Covered in Mud

*A Prayer from Psalm 51*

••

Jesus, please listen to my cries;
I must tell you my secret:
sometimes I do what is wrong
even though I know what is right.
I feel guilty, as if I'm covered in mud.
It's hard to tell you everything,
but I'm glad that I do.
Your forgiveness is like a bath—
all the dirt gets washed off,
and I am squeaky clean.

What a relief to let go of secrets
and let in your love—
a forever-love that smells so sweet
and never fades.

# You Never Leave Me

*A Prayer from Psalm 34*

When I look on your face, God,
I'm like the moon lit bright
by the dazzling sun.
Without your glowing warmth
I'm lonely,
lost in a long shadow.
I can't see anything!

Just when I think I've lost your warm light
and the shadows feel long and cold,
I remember that you never leave me!
You are close to anyone
with a broken heart,
beside us in dark places.
I will turn my face toward
your loving light.

# Where Are You, God?

*A Prayer from Psalm 42*

••

Where are you, God?

I need you

like a deer needs to drink from a stream.

I want to see you

the way crowds want to see a parade.

I am so sad

when I am without you.

My cries sound like thunder

in a rainstorm of tears.

I feel as if the ocean waves

are crashing around me

when the bullies tease me

and tell me you are not with me.

Where are you, God?
I long for you because
you are my help,
my hope,
my strength,
and my God.

# Is Anybody There?

*A Prayer from Psalm 142*

••

Where are you?

I'm going to say it again even louder:

Where are you?!

Is anybody there?!

No matter which way I look,

no one seems to care about me.

God, you promised!

You promised to take care of me

and keep me safe.

I'm begging you!

Don't just watch over me . . .

save me!

# A Lamp for My Feet

*A Prayer from Psalm 119*

••

God, let your scriptures be a guide

for me all of my days.

May they open my eyes,

so I can see your presence.

May they quiet my ears,

so I can hear your wisdom.

May they comfort my heart,

so I can feel your love.

May they bring me peace,

so I will not be afraid.

May they direct my lips,

so I may comfort others.

Like a bright light on a dark trail, O God,
let your words show me the way—
for your words are like a lamp for my feet
and a light to guide my path.

# Teach Me

*A Prayer from Psalm 141*

••

My mouth is like a door.
When it has mean or unkind things to say,
will you help me keep it closed, God?
Let only loving words come out.

My heart can choose what it holds close.
Help mine hold good things,
such as kindness, curiosity, friendship,
patience, and courage.

Teach my eyes to look for you,
even when darkness makes it hard to see.
I'll notice that you're next to me,
keeping me safe.

My prayer is like a candle.
It burns and crackles.
It rises up like smoke.
I hope it gives you the sweetest scent.

93

# Spring Comes Again

*A Prayer from Psalm 13*

••

Sometimes I feel as miserable as a dull gray sky—

or a jagged tree stump,

or the wind when it howls—

like someone who has just heard awful news

and cries, "No, no, no!"

Sometimes I worry

that you have forgotten about me

or that you don't hear me when I pray.

But then I remember the ways
you care for me, every single day.

I have a home and a cozy bed
and people who love me.

I remember that,
even after the longest, gloomiest winters,
spring always comes again.

And then I am thankful
that you are so good to me.

# A Song of Victory

*A Prayer from Psalm 118*

••

Dear God, you surround me,

front and back, right and left.

With you, I'm tucked inside

the perfect hiding place.

You defend me from trouble of every kind.

What can I do but sing a song of victory to you?

Your love is powerful.

Your love never fails!

Your love is wonderful.

It's as big as forever.

# Prayers of Creation

# We Are Your Creation

*A Prayer from Psalm 96*

••

God, you are spectacular!
You made the brilliant sky above me—
and the clouds that parade
and dance and twirl across it.
You made the rich, black dirt—
and the meadows whose flowers
are busy with bees and crickets and ladybugs
playing tiny symphonies for you.
You made the gigantic trees—
and the sturdy limbs that reach their arms
high into the air toward you.

You made the ocean,
the whales and fish and coral reefs,
and you made the mysterious sea creatures
that move deep down in the dark.
Everything in nature is full of gratitude
toward you and sings to you.
We are your creation, and we are beautiful—
just the way you made us to be.

# Rooted Deep

*A Prayer from Psalm 1*

••

How happy I am, from the inside out!

Knowing I belong to you,

I stand strong in this world,

like a sky-high tree,

rooted deep near sparkling waters,

green and alive,

bursting with the fruit of your Spirit.

I am not fooled by the empty chattering

of people who close their ears to you.

I listen instead for the sound of your voice

ringing out across the universe,

calling my name.

# God's Handprint in the Stars

*A Prayer from Psalm 8*

••

With your fingers
you created the heavens.
You hung the moon in the night sky,
and your handprint made the stars.

When I look up at the sky,
I see so many stars.
Sometimes they blink,
and other times they sleep.
I cannot count them.
They are like grains of sand
falling between my fingers.

We are like the stars.
You created everyone on earth,
and you know each of us by name.
We are as bright to you
as the stars in the sky.

And I wonder—
oh how I wonder—
how do you hold
all of us
in your arms?
Both one at a time
and all at once—
every minute of the day—
and still have room
to love us even more?

# When I Look Up

*A Prayer from Psalm 19*

••

When I look up at the sky, I see you—

your power,

your bigness,

your creative work.

You even made a home for the sun

so it can go from one side of the sky to the other,

touching everything with your warmth.

And when I read your Word, I see you too.

How wise you are,

how right you are,

how your Word continuously

refreshes me and gives me joy!

I pray that my eyes and my heart will always

be open to seeing even more of you!

# The Song the Earth Is Singing

*A Prayer from Psalm 29*

••

All of nature yells and sings:

*God is strong and beautiful!*

In the rainstorm I hear you, Lord.
In the falling *plop plop plop* of water,
in the crash and clap of thunder,
I hear your mighty voice.

I feel your strong rhythm in the forest.
The trees shake and twist like dancers.

This is the song all the earth is singing.
I sing it too:
*God, you are full of wonders!*

# Your Works Are Amazing!

*A Prayer from Psalm 104*

Creator of our Earth,
your works are amazing!
You covered the world
with the watery deep
and then carved the mountains
with rushing streams.
Just look at how
the flowing rivers
give life to the birds
that drink from them.

You made every blade of grass
grow to feed the animals
(and the humans too).
Just look at the ocean—
it's full of magnificent creatures,
big and small!
Throughout the land and seas,
I see the beauty of your Spirit
bursting through.
The earth is full of your creativity!
It is filled with wonderful works.
My heart overflows with the joy
of your creation!
I sing praise to
you alone!

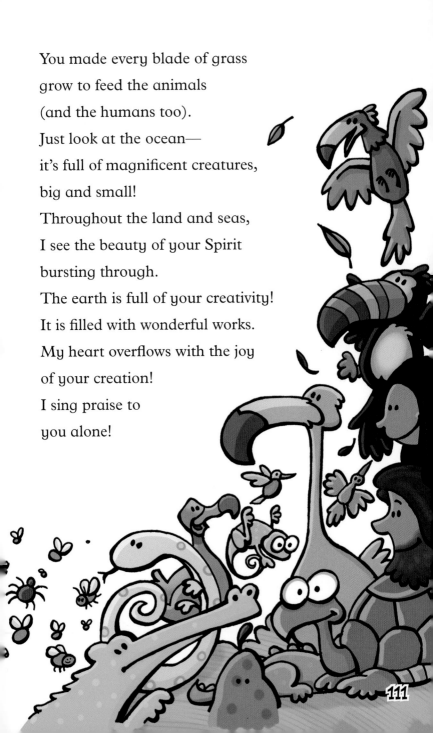

# You Make All Creation Dance

*A Prayer from Psalm 33*

••

I know you love to hear me sing
songs as sweet as a harp,
songs as joyful as a dance.
Thank you for giving me a voice to sing:

*You always keep your promises! You never let me down!*
*How mighty you are—your word made the heavens!*
*Your mouth breathed the planets, the sun, and the moon!*

You love when I sing of your beauty—
how you make all creation dance!
I fill up with joy and sing of your hope—
your love that lasts forever.

# You Made It All

*A Prayer from Psalm 46*

••

If giant waves crashed round the world
and snowcapped mountains fell flat as flat can be,
no danger made by nature or people
could keep me from knowing I am safe—
because you made it all,
every vast, incredible part!
You give me hope and courage to face anything—
no matter how scary, no matter how big.
The place I am safe
is in the center of your heart, O God,
like a tranquil island in a swift-flowing river,
safe from the world's storms.
Nothing can happen without you;
you make me shout with joy!

# The Earth Is Amazed

*A Prayer from Psalm 65*

••

Lord, I'm calling you Prayer-Answerer!

I'm calling you Giver of Good Things!

I've learned a new name for you: Bringer of Hope!

You have shown me all the great
things you've done.
You grow the food we eat
and fill the streams with the water we drink.

In the soft yellow glow of sunrise,
in the deep blue evening sky,
you are teaching earth your songs of joy!

Look at the hills and the meadows!
Look at the valleys!
They're alive with grain
and covered with flocks of animals.
They're singing and dancing to the song
you've taught the whole world.

This earth is amazed by you.
And I am too!

# All of Creation

*A Prayer from Psalm 147*

••

God, you are so mighty!
All of creation is made by you
and is known by you.

You have counted the stars
that burn in the night sky
and have given each one its own special name.

You paint the blue sky with clouds
and sketch perfect blades of
green grass on the hills.

You stir the breezes the way I stir dough
in a bowl with a wooden spoon.

Ravens with inky black feathers
and tiny, perfect eyes
call to you, and you feed them.

I put my trust in your unfailing love.

# Shout Hallelujah!

*A Prayer from Psalm 148*

••

Angels, sun, moon, and stars:

Praise the Lord!

Lightning, hail, snow, clouds, and stormy winds:

Praise the Lord!

God created them all!

Praise the Lord!

Mountains, hills, trees, animals, and birds:

Praise the Lord!

Kings and queens, presidents and principals:

Praise the Lord!

Young and old, kids and grown-ups,

babies and elders:

Praise the Lord!

All are close to God's heart.

Let heaven and earth shout,

"Hallelujah!"

# My Prayers

# My Prayers

# My Prayers

# My Prayers

# My Prayers

# My Prayers

The Spark Story Bible collection sparks faith in the lives of young children and families. Using kid-friendly language, colorful artwork, and vivid storytelling, these books take readers on a lively journey through God's Word.

Find out more at sparkhouse.org!